# THE THEOLOGICAL MUSEUM

for Don Paterson

Best wishes Paul

*For Sarah*

'. . . everything is ours – not mine –'
(Alexsandr Blok)

# THE THEOLOGICAL MUSEUM

## Paul Stubbs

### Foreword by Alice Oswald

# Acknowledgements

Some of these poems have appeared in the following publications:
*The North, Poetry Review, The Rialto, The Shop.*

A special thanks to the following people who have supported me
during the writing of this book: my mother and father, Jane
Griffiths, Bryan Howlett, Steven Mullan, Alice and Peter Oswald,
John Sayers, Rhiannon Shelley, John Wakeman and Mark Wilson.

First published in Great Britain in 2005 by Flambard Press
Stable Cottage, East Fourstones, Hexham NE47 5DX

Typeset by BookType
Front-cover image: sculpture by Jeff Midghall
Cover design by Gainford Design Associates
Printed in Great Britain by Cromwell Press, Trowbridge, Wiltshire

A CIP catalogue record for this book
is available from the British Library.

ISBN 1 873226 70 5

Flambard Press wishes to thank Arts Council England
for its financial support.

ARTS COUNCIL ENGLAND

website: www.flambardpress.co.uk

Flambard Press is a member of Inpress and Independent
Northern Publishers.

# Contents

# Foreword

These are great poems, with new things, both spiritual and simple, to communicate. They speak in a slightly different language, one that hasn't yet come about, with shifting grammatical rules and strange juxtapositions, making them exciting though occasionally difficult to read.

I admire their disregard for rhyme, assonance, conventional lineation and indeed anything that smacks of poetical correctness. Their poetic form is nothing more than a compulsion to speak broken up by a struggle with silence.

The Hungarian poet Janos Pilinszky said of his own poetry: 'It is a sort of lack of language, a sort of linguistic poverty . . . but in art each deficiency may become a creative force of high quality.' This is always the case with Stubbs's writing. The very awkwardness of the diction is the poem's transfiguring strength, something like the technical resistance great musicians work with and against:

> Yet now and again, out of nowhere,
> some form upon your flesh, it intrudes:
> an exit from your world
> it opens up
>
> – the doorway of an ear seems suddenly
> unending enough for you to enter into.

Stubbs is one of very few living poets whose work I come back to. He writes about the human body, which, under his pen, becomes the actual landscape of an afterlife:

> Who speak, as if your jaw, it was buried already
> underground: while the deaf above you, armed with
> spades, they wait, impatiently, to exhume
> it.

I hope that it is not untrue of any true poet that metaphor is the poet's own body-sense moving through the medium of language into something else, but no one before has been so aware of the human body as the very flask in which the change happens.

Alice Oswald

## When Writing a Poem

*'The writer can, without separating one from the other,
indicate the laws which govern each one of his poems.'*
(Isidore Ducasse)


Pick up your pen, as if it were a scalpel;
open up each day your own insides, remove

first any bones left over of the vertebrae
      of the selves that never quite
      managed to survive your drafts.

      From one poem to the next, always
keep at arm's length the bulk of the body
      of ideas you might use next.

Think of your imagination as nothing more
      than a labyrinth of intricate pulley-systems,
      fetching back and forth, each day,

      the unaging dummy-torsos that
      resemble you.

An ear for silence is essential; listen
      hard until it evolves, like a conch
      of permanent skin,

(it will enable you to locate the etymological
din of ancient poets, as they make their way
back over the flat white steppes of your page)

      to ascend up into heaven
      or back down into hell,
do this

by slipping up or down the bone-gears
      of your own spine.

At all times
    startle: introduce even a full-stop
with the surprise and aghast

        of your own severed head brought into
        your reader's room on a silver salver,

keep endlessly looking over
        and over your own form, and reject it:

        exercise those muscles now
that tomorrow you might well need as
        a post-world man.

Always hold your pen like a crucifix, but
        with a defiant air of non-
        religiosity;

while to keep track of your own creative
development,

        hang up upon the wall of your study,
like hunting trophies, those skulls of
        the poetical species you've
        evolved from;

        (imaginatively speaking
        of course!)

wear your own tongue like a tie askew –

And at all times, and in every single poem,
        flirt with God!
Do this by wearing your flesh like a low-cut
        strapless dress.

        And then, when finally
        you have nothing much left to say,
stop writing,

or when feeling like Proteus you begin to
stare off into the distance, distractedly
contemplating the shape
of all extraneous things.

So now after putting down your pen,
wait for something new and improbable to write
down again,

and then when having gone through the same
tried and trusted poetic routine,

for say, the next fifty years?
keel over and die,

rip out and rewrite every last blank page
of the sky . . .

# Purgatory

*For Alice Oswald*

'. . . *that the evil suffer most is*
*not true, their suffering is not*
*deep, in one sense it is a pleasant habit.*'
           (Edith Södergran)


Awoken this morning in my room by the
crackle of my small transistor radio

(playing the same old fiery tunes), I
weigh up my options for the day; get

dressed (in flesh) dust off (proudly)
the glass-case hung up on my wall, in

which sit two jaw-bones awarded to me
to commemorate the echo of my first

scream here in Hell. And in the monstrous
hours between waking and sleep,

feeling unwell, I retreat back into
the shadows of my ash-strewn room,
where feeling preposterously pious I read

out aloud from my char-black missal,

baptize myself in my own boiling tears,
and then pray, without hope, to no God.

Afternoons I do little but watch,
as those Gods who, in heaven, failed

to make the celestial grade, they bend
to bury the bones of their undeveloped race.

While from time to time, over a high-
pitched tannoy, a voice, it howls to
announce the next live event, which

today (incredibly) will be a public
autopsy on the body of Christ, which

along with all the other occupants
I'd dare not miss, watching this,

as, with unholy precision, Satan,
to rapturous applause, he removes
not one theological bone that could
or should be attributed to a God.

After an event such as this, unwittingly I weep,

before retiring to my room for no sleep.

Tomorrow, I will get up, get burnt, and then pray,
maybe, for the weather to relent;

and I will not, under any circumstances,
repent! – but will remember to scream.

# The Theological Museum

*For Mark Wilson*


Into the main front doors, look up to see it:
a palaeontologist's reconstruction of our God.

Above a table of theological
artefacts; such as the foetus
of an angel pickled in a jar;
and Satan's faulty thermostat.

Beside that, and to the right of the foyer, a block of wood
recovered from the Ark, where behind thick-tinted glass

all day it is sprayed by
the tears of the meek (to
keep it moist and to prevent
it from rotting away).

Walk further on, for the cross is here; and here
also upon a low flat ramp

the last charred fire-engine
to depart from hell, which
now parked here looks anything
but safe.

While inside the main hall, the murmurs of the crowd,
they begin to grow, for we are approaching the section

entitled WHEN GOD CREATED MAN.
For on display here is the prototype
of the very first human rib,
and beside it the lesser ribs,

once upon a time rejected, which, after strict theo-
logical tests, were deemed unfit to construct a race.

And past that (getting now
into the bowels of this old museum)
an aquarium containing the
souls God forgot to flesh.

Next to a phial containing the ashes of the hand-bones
of the last person to pray.

In the HALL OF OLD PULPITS
a preacher, out of nostalgia,
he wanders, shocked now seemingly
by his own silence, as

if he had only just had his script removed, and had now
no recollection of a tongue . . .

Into the evenings, a special-effects show, on which upon
a virtual-reality headset

the crucifixion is again
played out; and where from
one end of the corridor to
the next, you can hear it,

the collective wince, as the first of the four nails
is driven home.

Last in tonight (every night)
is the atheist, who, each day,
arrives to pay for the same
single attraction: a specially

constructed lab, where you (as a member of the public)
get to ignite a second hell,

which, let's face it, should be easy for any unholy
and

self-respecting wretch (or
so now the voice-over says).
So then to begin: take
hold

of your bible, your thermometer, and your match . . .

# Seascape

*For Sarah*


I remember when, as a child, I would run
back and forth along this beach. Hearing nothing
but the flapping of my own shadow,

like a weather-beaten canopy in the wind.
I would run, until there was no one else but me
on the beach, and my mouth like a shutter

had begun to bang and clatter on no words.
When I spoke, I could not be heard above
the collapse of the sea's cold scaffold.

I would listen instead to the grasses
upon the dunes. Those flailing green-cages
that refused to entrap a sound. Dumbfounded,

my voice would begin to cave in, like sand.
Burying me in my own silence. I would stand
in the same spot for hours, feeling nothing,

but the final sensation, of something lodged
inside the roof of my mouth, like a fossil
of what had once been my tongue.

# Head 1

*After Francis Bacon*


I did not see
the one who abandoned
me here. He was,
however, somebody who must have forced me
   to look up and follow
his departure into the sky. For I do
   it still –
And for that reason alone
   I am

unable now to turn my
head more than a few degrees either
to the left or to the
   right – When I speak my words they
   are whisked immediately
by my tongue into a scream,
                 a prayer.
   And with my head being
   only half-finished, it
seems that

   not even the curator of
   a theological museum would accept me
(preferring things as they
do to be *forgiven*, or, better still,
   unjustifiaby extinct) and
having of course only the one string
   attached, I can be no God –
   But what's left in this wire-cage, cubicle, void,
are no objects at all
   (though

it is not hollow)
– everything I say in here
does not come back to me. Like the head
    of a man who speaks only
    in echoes, I wait, each day, in vain
for the return of my always
    migrating jaw . . .
    – And it is just this
kind of restriction of space that so appals
    me. And so

    what else you might ask could
    be lying next to me? Only this:
a spirit-level containing Christ's
    own blood to keep me upright;
    that and a magnet
to keep the fragments of the few remaining
        planets in tow.
    – But everything here is
    in the wrong place

    – language here for me is
    not grammar, syntax, cadence etc,
    it is only my mouth
    deployed at such an angle, as to allow
    me to masticate on
only the most necessary of words;
    look up close at my neck
(not at thyroid, muscle, pulse)
    but at

    my veins circulating now with
the ink of the one who has most accurately
    described me. – An apostle or
        a saint maybe?
    But either way, there is no universe
        around me;
        this is it, the last
place to inhabit,
anywhere –

there is nobody else around
(though on my tongue dissolves
    still the body of the last
    person to ever see me).
Our lingua franca has evolved,
not because of my bestial gibbering, but because
    of the mouth of the body
    that has been reteaching me to speak;
    for my mouth

    it was broken-in originally
by the words of the Apocrypha. But at least
    now there will be no more
    talk of extinctions, last days,
    judgement etc.
And it is for these reasons alone
    that I am unable now
    to turn my head more than
    a few degrees

    either to the left or to the
    right.
For there was that time when somebody,
    he forced me to look
    up
and to follow his departure into the sky.
    That same somebody
    of course who once
    abandoned me here. I cannot remember
his name.

## Paraphrasing the Dumb

*For Jane Griffiths*

> *'Buried alive under the stars*
> *in the mud of night,*
> *do you hear my dumbness?'*
> (Janos Pilinszky)


So just how will you achieve it then, speech?
For the very first time, just how will a word

become less difficult? I mean look at you!
Struggling now to speak, as if a hook from one ear,
      it was attached, to lift it, your jaw,
      awkwardly, above your own form.

What about two pulleys on either side of your
face? To hoist up between your eyes, your mouth?
Or some many-jawed contraption designed by
      yourself
      to speak, if only, in echoes . . .

– But no, for you are an *untermensch*, grunting
and slavering in your own mouth-pen; so what
can you do then, the dumb, but rage?

To speak the words you have always wanted to,
      you would need to transform your head
      into that of a bull, or into that of
      an alligator,

      slumped in some naturalistic pose,
      and chewing on its own tongue . . .

But try at least to imagine it: your mouth
      as it speaks,

unlike the person born into a world of
perpetual silence: without jaw or tongue,
and ghoulish looking with no lips . . .

You who are dumb, and at an eternal
loss for words.

Who speak, as if your jaw, it was buried already
underground: while the deaf above you, armed with
spades, they wait, impatiently, to exhume
it.

And the world of course, for days on end,
it forgets you. Poor creature!

Was it perhaps then that the deaf, they abandoned
you here? Is it them that you see, each night,
in your dreams, as they push it, a tiny
cartload of your own mouth-bones over
some ledge?

But no, your perplexity at the world, it can
only ever now grow; sat there as you do, as if a
child, and picking at each word,

as if your tongue, it was a knife inspecting
the gristle upon a lump of raw meat –

But then, through an open window, an unidentified
shimmer: arriving like a visitation in your head,
that could, perhaps, be your voice?
But which sounds, to you,

as if a skyful of fish-birds, they were approaching,
or your own presence beneath your breath, it had
begun quite unexpectedly to flap . . .

A dream, a dream, yes, surely.
    For you have never quite managed to understand
human speech –

As hopeless as a blind man, attempting to construct
from a lone clump of clay, today, the exact proportions
        of your mouth,

you fumble, ungainly and haphazardly towards us . . .

    Maybe Christ, if he was prepared to, could
assuage your tongue with holy oils?
        But no, you will not speak, will not even
        dare to. – Neither a dialogue opened up with
        God or with yourself;

instead, in vain, foolishly, you tweak your ears,
like knobs, as if in search of some lost world's
                        transmission . . .

– So then your conversation, it will continue with
who?
With what beast or creature that will crawl in
close to converse with you?

    Yet now and again, out of nowhere,
some form upon your flesh, it intrudes:
        an exit from your world
        it opens up

– the doorway of an ear seems suddenly
unending enough for you to enter into.

# Soul

*'. . . what is it my soul feels?'*
(Pessoa)

Since your birth, I have lived here,
inside of you, your internal shadow.
Dreaming of the day, when (like a cripple
who runs off each leg-brace, mirac-

ulously cured) I'll run off finally,
the restriction of your human bones. Praying for you
each day, to quicken up in some
way the process of your own life.

Hoping for you, maybe, to flirt
a little with God, by dropping your flesh
like a dress from your shoulders;
as if by doing this you might be

able to swing it for me, my early
entry into heaven. But no, nothing to do but wait;
a prisoner behind flesh and bone.
While sometimes I sit, hand on chin,

just staring off into your within.
Imagining each nerve-end, as you breathe,
to be a grass-blade on some celestial plain.
And, though beneath you, you can-

not feel a thing. But imagine it,
my form lodged within each fissure
and every cleft. Where sometimes
I hide, when startled, suddenly seeing myself

by accident upon the backward mirror
of your eyes. – But something at least
to relieve this infernal human boredom.
And so this is how it goes on,

day after day, myself, a mendicant:
crouched down deep in your insides,
a shunned form, a form un-boned,
no use to your world.

## Paradise

Once here and settled you can do pretty
much as you please.

On arrival you are met at the top of this
dizzy altitude by your own personal angel,

(like the air's air-hostess) wielding both
ventilator and mask,

into which (though dead) you are told, for
an eternity, to breathe.

In a world where awkwardness has become extinct,
sudden movement of any kind is considered
an act of sedition,

but to incite only other more peaceful acts.

A geographical feature here is sign-posted
at 'God-level' (even when God isn't here),

as on earth, say in a desert, sign-posted
at 'Sea-level'.

You do not need money, all items remain
non-negotiable gifts.

Transport is quick and free; trains run every
second and every century,

hurtling souls across the designated tracks
of their old human bones.

If any solid ground appears, it is dispelled
at once beneath the weight of a saint's foot.

The main attraction here though is the all-
angled view of anything.

For all this, the thing you remember most
is on arrival (the moment after you have just died)
when you find yourself herded suddenly
into a small, yet amazingly bright room.

And where in the light you easily locate it,

your after-flesh slung like a coat across
a chair.

Our real flesh, that is to replace now the
flesh that restricts us and prevents us

from encroaching, just once, into nowhere . . .

## Prayer

Once I used to pray and hoped something
of my entire torso would be reborn; a limb maybe,
hoisted suddenly above me. But it wasn't.

Yet my mouth it floated. And my tongue it swung
like a hook with the corpse of each dying word;
for this practice did not seem very real.

And my palms, only just failing to touch, maintained
no holy connection with myself. There was
no inner-structure at work. And no answers . . .

And so now whenever I sit down for prayer,
all that appears in front of me is the air itself;
its inner-structure at work, its mechanics,

its conveyor-belts, reproducing clone after clone
of the same note of the same incomprehensible silence.

## Guidelines for Gods

Before even the holiest inkling of something,
such as a solar system or a wing,
first, to get up into your heaven, practise
your ascent by leaping from a wall,
a fence or anything
    a few feet off the ground.

Think only of weightlessness, or of a body forever
hurtling down the elevator shaft of its own soul.

Think big: for the construction of your new
celestial home, use only a surveyor's plans
    for an astrologer's dream-city.
    Create it in conjunction with
    no known geometry.
A place earmarked only for those destined
    for immortality;

which, pretty much, will be like living anywhere,
but without solid ground or lungs . . .

    Sat at your translucent desk
    sketch out a series of apocryphal
    yet believable stories to con-
    vince each new acolyte
of the future of their past, call
    it: a bible.

    Next, pick up a rib, any size;
    construct the first member of
your new race.

Ensure always that he or she or it
    resembles your own image

(do this by stretching the flesh of your face
in your imagination, over and across each soon-
to-be constructed skull).

Remember: holiness and love must remain
your main themes. Pleasure being
all that you sing, and with
every second the anniversary of the joy
you bring.

Though (playing it safe) best to obtain for yourself
a diary, if only to felt-tip in with a marker-
pen those days on which you most
want to be (officially)
celebrated.

Angels? Yes, lots of them.
Design the anatomy of each as you might
a physical representation
of a God like you,

out of only the most improbable
cartilage, muscle and sinew.

Name some saints, make up a list of possibles,
some hymns also that your new race *will not*
be able to hum in their heads.

And just to make a game of it,
excavate a place out of the core of your new
planet, where everything in-
human might reside, call it:
hell. Populate it with those
members you deem 'unfinished',
clothe them using anything left over of that

huge stockpile of flesh that
you used to create your first
race, think of them as evil.

And then finally,
        on those days when you are
        unable to see past your own
        self-importance, ask your-
        self again, just how will you justify not answering
to every plea for help, every 'Why?'

        (On every other day)

        check if you can still look
        yourself in your own eye.

# Silence

*For John Wakeman*

Since childhood, it has been infatuated
with the sound of my voice.
I notice it swallow the words
the instant that I speak.

Days are, it will flit like a fly
about a word that has already died.
In a crowded room, it has
an absolute hatred for all those

awkward moments in conversation
when nobody speaks. Each hour
it searches in vain for some brand-
new sound. As, overweight with

platitudes, it grows more and more afraid
of boredom. So close to me,
this microclimate of movement
under the lens of my most scrupulous eye

and, though pliable to the core, it reveals
no outward sign of transforming,
though it can be seen to wince
when face to face with itself

in the mirror of both of my glaring eyes,
as if it had just bitten down hard
upon the length and breadth of its
own tongue. While its impalpable self,

it now sways from side to improbable side
to the rhythm of these words.
Until, hunched and pensive on all fours,
it will begin to prey again,

from dawn to dusk, on some
unsuspecting tremor, while counting out
my heartbeat, using an abacus
in a free hand.

# Sin

Who wonders what you are then if not
a sinner? If not a sinner, then what?

A dancer? Under the fixed death-silence
of the moon, feeling oppressed not by it
      but by your own soul trickling
      like a slack thread of sweat
      across your brow –

You are a moral trapeze act, performing
each day your autecological gymnastics;
      a creature or a something suspended
      above your own form on hooks . . .

as if in a perpetual yet all too human
state of ascension . . .
      And God won't see
your kind of humanity, sat in groups
in some lost hinterland of the soul –
      didn't you know? –

like old hags stiching together sacks,
as makeshift lungs for the afterlife –

What the hell! Your banishment in your
darkest hour is only yourself, and
the same single choice, each night, you
awake to: Remember?
      God, with two outstretched fists
      and with only the one soul-preserving
      palm to pick from –

neither the last charred rib of Satan,
nor the nail.

A choice then between the pit and the
spit in the trough of your dryed-up
angelic tears . . .

So imagine then what you could have been
if not a sinner? No? For with the taste

of the dirt already in your mouth of your
own unknowable hell, it's hopeless (isn't
it?) this gloom that perpetuates, that
          blazes, forces you to sit, each
          day, for your own entertainment,
          and watch

as your ashes, they are poured through
a never emptying hour-glass. By whom?

And your own form has changed because
of it.

Go to a priest, hand him each word
as if a bone, and like a palaeontologist
he'll inform you of what you once
          were.

– Like a surgeon performing immense
and improbable and Godless operations,
          he will remove your soul
          like extraneous scar-tissue,

put it in a jar and tell you to go
home. But then to stare at what
          else?

You who are the unredeemable, who
enjoyed the Apocrypha more than the
actual bible,

hummed the introit before
the banquet held in celebration
of your own flesh and blood –

You who are the sinner, who shall
not now be all his power and glory:

For you are his other face,
the religious form born out of interpretation;
the last of the hereditary
men of sin, born out of Adam's
gross indecision,

and with a thin protruding bone sticking
out now from your palm, where the nail
would have been . . .

– Watching them then, without envy, the
saved, as they begin their mass migration
from their very own shoulder blades . . .

While your head, it topples like a rock
from the flank of the pit crumbling in-
side. – And you are less and less equipped
now to deal with your own demise;
you who are straining now only for
the scent of your own rotten flesh,

stood here dumb and cold: though the
home-fires will be long kept burning . . .

'I have sinned' admits you, the sinner.
No true or false God unargues.

Where finally, crouched down now onto
your haunches, you pray, away among
no pews . . .

– You now that no longer resemble a human:
or not quite yet, a biblical beast.

# A Pilgrimage

*For Steve Mullan*

*'And I shall be useful when I lie down finally.*
*Then the trees may touch me for once, and the*
*flowers have time for me.'*
(Sylvia Plath)

Stood at your gravesite, today.
The wind filled my breath.
I read out aloud a few of your
poems. All day long I sat there among
the rough countryside and flowers I cannot name, watching
where time had finally settled.

The sun
as if on the threshold of touching, never quite;
only its ghost like a fine density of time
barely scraping against the small church windows.

There is a horror
in the space of fields, yet a look of immeasurable
calm appears on every slabstone, when the sun eventually falls.
The grass like a voice just out of hearing
flails in and out of itself, to nowhere, a carriage
of some new green objectivity. The wind moves off.

Then evening from between the trees
finds out my mind, suddenly like a match lit
in some dark cellar or attic.
Tells me it's time to go.
And I can go now, now that
I know for sure you've been granted your wish.

And that you're finally happy.
I'm glad, not sad like I thought
I would be. And it's true now I know.
We're all alone. I saw myself here dead.
And everyone else too.

With that in mind I leave,
with crows sinking upward to the bottom of the sky.
Where its heavy red canopy lends to the hilltop
now a jacket. The hills tingle with the
faint rumble of thunder, as the sky
for a second jams, then frees away.

# I Look Up At an Icon of Christ

*Sacré-Cœur Basilica, Paris*


and immediately and unashamedly assume
the weight and the shape of his own
proportions. (God's artificial limbs.)

I with my shy stare that sidles out
from a cleft in my chin, looking and listening
to the prayer of a priest on marble;

the echo of his every word, like an
undistracted and repetitious ghost, speaking
in time from some impalpable world.

The silence in here, something seen –
(a field now of chopped-off tongues
Christ himself runs his palm through) –

as I look back up into the light
that appears to emanate from his own eyes;
until my own body as if an obelisk,

it feigns the effect of a sundial,
allows my own outline to cast not the slightest
shadow of a doubt on his existence;

on his demeanour, poised now and
seemingly at the ready to restyle my weight;
to leave now his own presence

like the shadow of my own shape.

# Absence

Absence: I sometimes see it this way.
As myself minus heart, flesh and soul.
A structure, an ungainly
yet elusive whole.

I X-ray its polymorphic shape with my stare –
it reveals only my face, vacuous, looking there.

It is like a shadow in which its presence
has already left.

Even now as close as the sky
and as far away.

When it arrives it shuts down time:
leaves a stone clock-face on my wall.
It is always moving and always
perfectly still;

it is a place of religion, where all
those who are lost go.

It is the absent priest in his open-air church
speaking his wordless versicle

to his congregation who answer back with nothing
but faraway looks and silence.

How do we become its most recent neophyte?
By not remembering the affection
or friendship of others.

By always looking with awe into its
most despotic eye,

as if into a dazzling yet improbable
corridor of mirrors,
which will install us as its chief
                    (only) illusion.

It is omnipresent: a mountainous backdrop
of nothing into which my own features
are carved.

It can be found at no known
or fixed address:
you can find it in an empty field
and in a deep hole.

Absence: I sometimes see it this way.
As myself minus heart, flesh and soul.

## The Sower

Walking through these cornfields
with the improbable sun rising,
and with no objects around
but the three solitary crows,
like shadows of your own hand.

At times here your eyes seem
like nail-heads,
wanting to impale something
palpable from
the never-ending spaces.

You have walked into the corn
as if you were treading waist-deep
in water, or awkward
and unbalanced you were ploughing
through on stilts.
The field flailing all about you.

Your hand emerging like a rake
from your coat pocket.
As the field sets sail suddenly
with a hundred born-butterflies
into the bad light
and you release the remainder
of the seeds.

While at night you dream
how each seed you sowed
might grow by the next day
into something unimaginable
like heaven,

more beautiful
and longlasting than your life,
something
quite unaccustomed to erosion
or actual dying.

# Apollo: Ascent from Earth, Universal Order

*After Dante*


It was him, juggler of the planets,
sleight-of-hand magician of souls.

Who is the universe, both its dark
side and its light;
who had created the
things I saw, so soul-shockingly bright.
I peered over and beyond
the balls of my own eyes to witness it,
this astrologer's city,
echoing with the din of
such all-consuming light,
it burst throughout the diaphanous nook
and cranny of every-
thing,

producing an unexpected decline of
my own outline . . .

For moments here are
remembered too quick, as if two
phases of your own skull
were always in eclipse;
as your body, it is spun
off into the airless air.
And what I saw I became, inaccessibly
transformed into the
body of anything,

like being suddenly inside of, and opening unexpectedly
the eyes of, a lifeless marble white statue.

And then through sheer
possessive exultation, teaching it to sing,
for every presence here
sings as if in echoes; a polyphonic society
of two-tongued things.

O Apollo,
for the prize of your laurel,
pass on to me your own power,
leave me feeling never once
exhausted, a living portent
only of exceptional truth.

As if suddenly I had been created like you:
out of only the most improbable materials.

Allow me, from at least
one peak of the muses, if not both,
to look out on all I see
in mind-splitting ecstasy.
With my soul flashing back
your light like a lake does the earthly midday sun –
and from on top of these
great dizzy heights,
allow me to breathe, to breathe,
but have no lungs . . .

Come into my form, the
opposite of how you approached the problem
of Marsayas; reflesh me,
journey until within a
lens-breadth of my eye,
until your stare becomes recognizable to
my very own skull-bones.
O Apollo, anachronistic
form of every known world,
hurl your presence like a lampshade across my shape,
allow your bright holy
light to cast off from me a thousand of your like-
minded forms,

alternate the size of me,
that I might then resemble the shape
of your own chosen tree –

construct for me from its
foliage, as strong as that
of an eagle's nest, a triumphal crown,
both too big and too small
for any human head, such as
that of Caesar or a poet –

but to be crowned with love,
not shame, as you hand it to
me, O Delphic God, your Peneian bough.

From the greatest flame
follow smaller, less influential flames,
but flames nonetheless
that might light up the words of a prayer
read even in darkness or
from on top of the peaks
of Cyrrha at night.

The brightest light here
reverses the natural angles of things;
so that they do not shine
in any one single way; three-quarters of the sky
veering at the point of
the celestial equator, so
that the resultant horizon, it intersects,
where the ram, weightless,
etheric form, floats free . . .

and then looks back at me,
as the brightness of each
star, it is increased, brilliantly outshining all others;
thus on apparent display
the natural world sets its mortal course for the heavens.

With its doorway facing east,
as evening there hidden behind
unearthly crystal-mist, it glimpses heavenly premonitions
of the darkening hemisphere.

As I turned then suddenly
and startlingly back into the sun of Beatrice's face.
It was noon sharp, and
reflections from her face showered me in stares,
too bright even for an eagle
to fly up close to, but
fly I did, like a pilgrim
but from ear to ear in
search of a sound, a sense to magnify my arrival here.

But only the pupilless white
eyes of each angel could bear to look on,
though my imagination's eyes they strained
in vain to . . .

Along this way, where each
and every entity, it moves;
those especially it seems
most theologically motivated, who dare always to move
beyond mere mortal possession.
Bodies that wheel, so bright
and so knowing,

it's as if, every split-second,
they were adjusting to 'truth'
the setting on some God-built
implant called 'paradise' inserted inside their brains;
as they moved both upward and
horizontally into another day,

into another sun's rising
above no visible horizon.

And there amid all this
stood Beatrice, staring off into that final sphere,
where the circles
in speed, they are increased,
as if some eternal fair-
ground ride, whose speed,
it is said, is meant to pin you to its innermost sides,
and then to hold it, your
weight there forever . . .

While staring at this,
I stared on at her, and
like Glaucus consuming the food that gave,
unbeknown to him, the
sustenance to his next-
to-follow-form, I gorged down the comprehension
of all that I saw.

But now no words
like carriages will fetch and carry us back
from the other side
of humanity; only
he, who first inflated the lungs of me,
who shadowed my ear
with his word, and created in the spheres
where the circles are
most obviously decreased the origin of
all natural things.

Only his ongoing example of things can be understood . . .

Here, where the sky
like a novelty of space, untouched by the plough
of human exertion, like
soil eternally unworked,
contests the right to
forever drift uninhibited. And with no slow-
thicket of cloud in which to hide,

so much so did its
unhurrying beauty compel me to groan out loud
in the pain of happiness
that the only sensation I felt inside me was
the agitation to
witness it now some
more,

this sky like water across which skim souls
like stones thrown by
some exultant God.

As mouth agape I stood
staring, as she beside me, already beginning to speak,
she uttered these words,

'See all of the entities here, not by
using earth's false accuracies of sight,

do not attempt in ungainly human
ecstasy
to roll away your eyeballs, as if
in an attempt to skittle the bones
of anything perceptible that moves,
merely enliven
the surface of each thing,
not as
lightning would on earth,
but up here
as a
soul does by tracing only the one
outline
of God.'

If any change occured in my demeanour
after she had said this,
it was only to adjust my gait into the
position of someone even
more perplexed.

And so then I replied,
'If before I seemed
in a state of human exultation, it was because
I felt too overjoyed,
tongue-tied in wonder,

like a child standing
upon a shore seeing for the first time the ocean;
as up here the brazen
sky it lapped and lapped at the shores of my soul.

Yet now, feeling even
more perplexed, I wonder just how am I to pass
safely on into and beyond
these upcoming conditions of fire and air.'

Then looking at me in the way
that a mother does her insuppressible and naive
child, she said,

'Seek not to find here
any individual form shaped of its own accord,
but linger longer with
your stare, until you
see in each construction only the construction
of God; for every object
here, no matter how outwardly different from
another, arrived from the
same single design and
thus bears eternally that
imprint.

Each form steers its course
over the great sea of being-
fully-sailed, and with God both at its helm
and on high lookout
for any irreversible changes
in this sea's conditions.

This is how all creatures
endure themselves, how they motivate each other
to enforce the design even
of the earth itself –
And it is love that binds them;
they that are iron-filings
to God's magnet, intellect
the design of that magnet.

All stares of eternal sight
arrow towards the one target, all these creatures
are destined to hit the one
spot; though when any of them
through eternal unresponsiveness or unGod-like
love misses this one spot,
then they are destined only
to fall, no more than animals back down to
their own primal earth.

And so if what I say is true,
then the wonder should have drained out
of you, as if water from a
basin,

for your ascent should feel
now commonplace, God's natural gravitational pull,
leaving you joyfully weight-
less, as if from your own soul's elevator shaft
your body had been suddenly
dropped.

And so finally, remember that
the earth, yes, also is a flame, but only in its stillness,
in its grounded weight of light.'

Then turning away from me,
she turned back again to face the sky.

## Listening to Music: Beethoven's
## Piano Sonata No.14 in C Sharp Minor


A sudden immobilization. Until beauty,
the shadow of my insides, arrives, and I assume
a second, more imperceptible form. For

this is the music of inanimate things,
allowed suddenly to flex unused muscle –
like the saved man in heaven allowed for

the first time the use of his now celestial
limbs; and rejoicing in this, his first
improbable dance. – A redemption for the

lunar soul, in this his finest piece.
With each note a moonstone re-entering
the atmosphere of my own inscrutable hearing.

It is Beethoven himself, up on the moon,
looking back to ponder my own listening;
from that earless world, where no sound is ugly.

And this is the music that now fills up
my room: a sound functioning after sound,
as if the piano itself had grown extinct;

but where the music, pianoless, plays on:
abandoning me here now its final pair of
ears: Beethoven's only human headphones.

## Young Girl Playing Violin, Evening . . .

She stands, stunned, as
if in shock, amid the rubble
of the applause that has
just fallen down all around
her.

Her face producing a kind
of pre-world stare . . .

Before she begins again,
sweeping away the notes with her bow,
her elbow, an ordered end
to the silence resting
briefly beneath her chin.

The sound of the strings so tuned to her within,
as if stretched across the violin were her very
own nerve-ends . . .

For increasingly beautiful,
the music demands of me now a more advanced,
non-human way in which to
listen.

So that for a moment then,
my hearing-self it migrates,
leaving only my deaf-self
here finally in a state of
absolute abeyance: while my eyes,
they look on, straining,

hoping to seek out new ears in the dusk.

# The Anatomy of the Saved

*'Upheavels of flesh and spirit,*
*disorders at high altitudes.'*
    (Juan Ramon Jimenez)


The anatomy of the saved cannot be
distinguished from those damned by

any one single human characteristic;
such as hair-colour, facial-features,
               temperament, or eyes. For
               even Christ's body and all
who saw it on earth could not tell
       the difference.

(A surprise then, perhaps, that the
               sponge soaked in vinegar
was not carried to the
               lips of the wrong God?)

               For hung up on his cross,
even he himself, he must have prayed
               (like any human would) for
               the pulse of an alternative
               heart to start;

for bodies up here, in heaven, suspended
               as they always have been,

between the faraway flesh of earth and
the close, unseen proximity of the soul,
               they experience it, each day,
               the sudden sharp pang of bone;
a reminder then, maybe, that every entity
               here,

               at one time or another, they
               miss it,

being human – the fallibility
and the uncertainty of what, if anything,
might occur.

Yet one day, so far in
the future, when some archaeological
dig turns up both the
ungainly and triple
vertebrae of the father, the son,
and the holy ghost,

when both man and God have become extinct,
just where then will these bodies be housed?

What God will be in place then to account
for them all?

Abandoned and left as the next
species of man on earth will be, to roam,
unconsciously free again of the knowledge
of sin.

But for now up here, these
bodies, they dance and spin, as if
neck-deep within water, or
as if choreographed by a butterfly
not God; and without any
obvious outline or volition, and

as if always having recently
slipped the leash of their old human skin.
– While their God, he watches
them, their muscle-free
anatomy,

their dancing, awkward and unsightly,
when set against the theology
of his pure presence.

## Acolyte

What have you got to do here then, to join?
To be allowed entry into this lame and con-
                        fectionary mindset,

this swing-door church to book in and out of?
And its door suddenly, a sky wide-open, waiting
        for your God to close it, and
        to push back across the bolt,

        before who gets back in? So just
who now are you turning your back on,
        yourself? What, some kind of
                        resurrection?

            Yes, but a transformation
            kept personal, and well within
            the timetable of flesh. (In
            your mind at least.)

– Something involving levers and cables
                    certainly, and yes,
                    maybe even a handle
to jerk you suddenly bolt back upright
into the abrupt and instantaneous bone-
                    chair of your original
                    form . . .

            And at some stage of
        course, you will be needing to pray;
        so for now, go on then, borrow these,

            these old flesh-gloves,
        so as to hand-imitate your own
                    abstract and unpraying
                    palms . . .

But at the base of whose feet now are you
                    crouching?
What future icon will not now be able to
feel your tears upon its cheek?

        But so pious here, and so silent,
        as if you were crouched down now
        at the graveside of your own
                    mouth-bones,
and
on which now, dumbstruck, you lay a rose . . .

– But who exactly was it gave it to you, this
book? Is there inside, maybe, on any page at
        all, some sacrificial killing? One
        carried out on only the most endurable
        of your species?

        (A species that does not gauge death
merely by the thickness of the dust-levels
        upon its skin.)

        So try not now to imagine it then:
        the burial of a three-spined thing.

        For could you or anyone else be
truly expected now to remove it, the image
        of the shape of that coffin-size
        from your head?

        No! of course not, or the amount
of dirt that would be needed . . .

So what kind of creator made you? You
        here with your patched-up theology,
        and second-degree sin.

                A creator who, before
        your birth, must have lifted it,

his image, like a mask, from off
your chin.

– And so what if by accident, then, all this
time you had been reading the *wrong* book?
That inside that phylactory that you carry
about on top of your head

was contained only the parchments
of a world where you yourself are
already dead? And where now only
shadows hold sway,

and where not one of them has ever
actually crossed themselves (enacting instead
some never-before-seen design across their
chest)?

No?

Well maybe if you were to just pick
up now that glass of blood sat there upon
the table (while attempting now not
to draw breath and inflate the lungs
of the you that might just baffle
death).

– So go on then, drink it, wash away now any
incongruous self left inside,
both those bodies with bone-structures and
those bodies without . . .

But where, here and now,
the taste of a final body upon your
tongue, it dissolves:
dissolves and refuses
to resist,

– the impression here finally that very
soon one of you will no longer exist.

## Eternity

I am already in front of you and
far behind.

I shimmer a mirage of spaces,
or like a cathedral, where inside you will find
only other more sacred spaces.

You cannot, though, mark your
own progress by me – look at me, then look away.
I'll be a different presence
you're forgetting.

But visionaries have at times imagined
that they've seen me.

When sometimes I would hunch
into the stump of a tree on the horizon.

As if in disguise, hiding awhile
from those writers,
who, from the outermost edge of space,
attempt to coax me,

by leaving a trail, a few titbits
of their most original lines.

But even if stood two inches away,
even if so close, I became enlarged
in the close-up sphere of their eye,
they couldn't see me –

There can be only the one way.

So now young poet, move not further away,
come closer still. – Let us break down the barriers
that have existed between us.

Allow me, just for a second,
the use of your body,
allow me (to gain my balance)
the use of your gait.

Sell me (for a fair price) your weight
in flesh, your soul, your heart
and limbs too;

and I'll come (I promise) crawling, walking,
running to meet you.

# When Selecting a God

*'. . . must we wait for a God, and which one?'*
(Karin Boye)


First, underline, with a steady hand, those
parables and stories in each of the different
bibles that you could, if forced to, believe.
Then removing your human eye, replace it with
the eye-piece of
                    a telescope reversed;

so that even your own body (seen by your soul),
it will already be so far away from you.

Decide, at once, whether or not to seek out
an alternative planet (somewhere unknown to
                    those who breathe), or if an
                    atheist, and uncertain how
you might well look in some new celestial
                    home

(when alone and in front of your own bedroom
                    mirror),

                    cross-dress by trying on
                    the chasuble of a priest! while remembering
                    (at all times) to apply
                    the necessary cosmetics
                    until you yourself have
begun to resemble the complexion of some-
                    body 'saved'.

                    Next, construct for yourself a cross,
one large enough so that either you or a friend can
                    gauge just how much human suffering
                    is required to become a God.

Compare it only with the suffering of Christ upon his cross,
when, as if stretched out upon a rack of his own bones,
                    any encroachment, out of himself, towards
                    home,

                    tightened only further the pain . . .

But once you have selected your God, then pray:
                    lay out your mind before his
                    or her eye, until it becomes
                    as exposed and as accessible
as that of the bones of the carcass of a fowl
                    upon a table after a meal.

Do not say your prayers over the telephone
or attack any false idol in private
                    (even those holy images inside
                    that have long since condemned
                    you).

While to draw in the crowds, now to this, your
                    first place of worship,

                    attach realistic yet fake plastic
                    tears to the eye of each and every
                    icon. While then, for the duration
of your mouth, spread the word,

                    that miracles happen (almost) every
                    other week here at your local church!

And so now, suffering from no apophatic remorse,
                    and when now

                    your God, he is firmly set in place
                    and looking out over his entire kin.
                    Be prepared (still) to not know
where to ever truly find him,

explaining (in an always opaque way)
to non-believers

'that on his exact whereabouts I really cannot
say, only that he or she will be
both

as close to you and as faraway as sin'.

So finally check now more closely then,
feel how much of you is left still
beneath your own skin.

# The Wind, Pared-Down

The wind, pared-down
        to a presence
by the longing
        in both my eyes.
A faraway voice
        emerging
from each tree. If each tree
        is a thicket
of inert tongues.

When walking into or out
        of it,
it divides as if it were
        a waterfall,
or the sense of my flesh
        as curtains
that allow me through.

And so effortless
        and so pliable
in every joint.

It has become almost
        my second shadow,
which, impalpably
        at least, reflects
my every other move,

        relocating its double
in my amorphous
        and tactile gait.

Remaining in this improbable
    state. Until,
    by listening
to the rustle of each tree,
    it comes to realize
that it is that self, now
    waist-deep in green,
treading leaves . . .

It is itself, now
    the noise that
    it is hearing.

## Frozen

There are no signs of life here –
this being the after-effect of ice.
It is the countryside chipped out

from chrystal; where the animals
and trees, like objects postponed,
are exhibited as imperceptible forms

in January's only display-case.
There are insects solid in snow,
like premonitions of themselves,

and myself nearby on the road,
feeling fragile, and at any second
as if I might suddenly shatter

into a thousand perfect pieces. So then
I dare not move, like each of the other
living species that linger here;

I have been entombed by my own shadow
and my outline is slowly changing,
as if through growing cold

I could eventually find myself,
disfigured, redesigned, and forced
to meander, an eternity, inside

the museum of my own sensations.

## Preparations for the Afterlife

*'Meditate on what you ought to be in body*
*and soul when death overtakes you.'*
            (Marcus Aurelius)


At the beginning of each day, either
    meditate or pray,

        until all of your human form, it has begun
        to stray absently from your mind.

        Exercise regularly,
by raising your torso, until your body
        no denser than your soul, or weighing

more now, it seems, than your heart,

it has begun to attain the stance
needed to fly off from yourself!

        Practise walking off the edge of things,
        walls, cliffs etc,

maintaining your footing in midair by
always believing in the vacancy of its
        once solid ground –

        Remember, in heaven, being so bright
        your eyes will be white,

                        so
(ignoring all health warnings)

                at every opportunity
stare directly into the naked sun; until your pupils,
                like black stones,

        they disappear, at once, into
        the small white lake of your eyes.

67

Think of your human design
as no more than that of some celestial
         sundial

    that might, suddenly, at any time,
    reveal to you, on some adjacent wall,

            the shadow of your final
and all-conclusive form;

    take one less breath each day,
    until your lungs have permanently deflated:
         do this,

            until you
have learned how to breathe without them –

    In front of the mirror,
adjust and re-adjust your gait into

    the position of someone growing
    ever more amazed and perplexed

            by what they see . . .

If it helps, obtain from your local
                 library the
following books:

    a study on morphology, eschatology,
    anatomy, and/or a series of the most

    basic theological texts . . .

            Symptoms of the saved
            on earth?
Any random or overwhelming impulse of love
            for mankind,
    characterized by a lack of consciousness
            of the heart,

growth of a second tongue, and/or spinal
imbalance,
culminating in a startling yet imperceptible
new evolution of
your gait . . .

prepare and study like this for that
most special destination,

until when, at last, your God, he has
begun the painstaking process of freeing
your own soul

(as if he were skinning
an animal),

imagine him
cutting up from under your loins

and then pulling it, your skin, out from
under your eyes,
joints and genitals,
until with both hands
you yourself can help by grasping

hold of all of the remaining connective
tissues . . . until

from within, each limb of
the post-world you, by him,

they have been pushed through,

out into that alternative world
of no-bone, muscle or sinew . . .

So now, finally then,
yet for the first time, practise waking

while you are still asleep, grow
atoned . . .

## Visitations of the Deaf

I wonder just what it is that forces
you to believe that you can actually
            still hear something?

Is it the 'you' inside perhaps that
you imagine grows increasingly more
            susceptible to sound?

– No; for surely a God of silence, he
must have created you? One, perhaps,
            with cleft hooves,

who does nothing, forever, but bask
like the blest in the reflection of

            his one functional ear . . .

until then, once more, you believe
that you might just have heard it,
            your own voice,

as if an echo-man and wearing your
own ears as headphones and attempting

to speak (always) in time to your own
            incomprehensible words;

            the world observing you,
as you flail your arms like a madman
above your head, as if in some last-
            ditch attempt to rid

yourself of all of the
unheard words that buzz
like flies about you.

*

(People watching you and laughing as you
struggle to straighten it, your own skull,
            as if an invisible crown.)

            And there is a natural surrender
to all this; an endless giving up of the
            ghost;

            as, each day, alone, you walk
            into it, the etymological ruins
            of your own interior world

(having escaped now all of its word-laws,
the imposed limits of language set by

yourself, which, through either eternal in-
articulation or by gratuitous self-verbal

attacks, have forced you here today to sit,
perpetually, like some silent nonentity,

            awaiting a first set of ears . . .

and while swallowing forever the last
of the remembered words in your head).

            A landscape of switched-off
            microphones; with each species
a mannequin wheeled up close to every one

            (the bodies outside of you
you believe are only really the shadows of the
            real speaking people inside)

as, each day, you wade,
knee-deep, throughout
your own self-humanity . . .

*

– And then, from this, to the torso-by-
torso procession outside on the street;

the one kind of speaking
race who, when silent, do

not carry you, an earless dummy of them-
selves, on into their minds.

But it does seem that of

all the different races who communicate
through silence, your body, it has been
chosen as *the* prototype.

– So maybe right now, on some alternative
planet, your body, it is the wafer placed

upon the tongue of some
alien and mute species?

So just what could your own world here be
then? –

this place that makes you want to alter
the design of every mouth that you see,
as if wet clay, until you have constructed
one that you yourself can
hear . . .

embalmed as you are
by your own silence,

and seeing only premonitions of yourself
        hearing words

        (that are only really the
        flash-points in a continuous
dream-sequence).

        *

So have you, I wonder, even yet woken
        up?

For try and try as they might, each morn,
no bird has ever yet managed to wake you! –

(you imagine each bird as if a whistle
with the ball removed from its throat).

– But now, standing here, like some in-
        vulnerable and ungainly
        beast,

you yearn to visit just one last place
where you might be able to hear something;
        but just where remains
        for you to go?

        Nowhere! that's where.

        And so now finally you
go there, swinging yourself up and round,
yet always back to the base of your own
        heel,

        as if an internal
yet always non-moving acrobat onto the pole
        of your own spine . . .

trying to loop, lip by lip, into a verbal world,
attempting, in vain, to leave your old one behind;
    but neither yourself nor your
    mind can manage to escape it.

So,
instead, you stand and stare, deep into your
own interior glare; while shouting out over
and over again for your own hearing-torso

    to return; for it to emerge
    back finally from the 'all'

this torso, that has never yet managed to
meet you, any time that you have called . . .

# Fragments of a Crucifixion

## I. CHOSEN

Where prayer has deboned you, and your
jaw, it has been dislocated by the Word,

you kneel down upon your own prie-dieu
(praying for yourself to follow you).

You, like a figure of origami built up
                    out of your own parchments

                    (fearing one match struck
                    might ignite and undo all
                    of your good work)

and looking out now past all of the
heads here before you,

you consider every clod of earth that
protrudes even a centimetre above the
                    ground, a tumulus in which
not one of your own family has been
                    buried –

                    I wonder then what planet
                    you believe you are on?

Here where the larynx of each being,
it opens only to pronounce the saved
                    (the tongue a decoration),

                    making you what then?

For it is not that you are feeling
lost exactly, or a long way from home, no,

but with creatures in grass-hats on
paralytic stools adapting better to

    this world than you,
it is clear then that you are lacking
        a true definition of yourself –

You who in appearance look like you
are continually tensing yourself for something;
as if your head, it was placed upon the
        block of your own shoulder blades,

    but to determine the weight of
    just whose hand poised above
           you?

    As you grimace and strain to
    attain your most iconic face,

but with your rapture, as yet, only
    shoulder-high,

    it is a case for now of simply
    burying it, your icon beneath
    the ashes of some burnt-down
        world,

that or attempt here finally to run
off the leg-braces of your own bones . . .

    Yet still to pacify an absence
        you resist,
waiting instead for some sign in the
        sky:

    for something eternal to be
    projected back here through
        the universe,

    by mirrors biblically arranged . . .

## II. CRUCIFIXION

But orphaned here and stood
next to what exactly, an angel?
Yes, and holding outside of
its chest, your lungs, long
since spent of all breath . . .

But still you cannot say it,
can you? The name of your creator,
                              no!

Until then, yes, once again you
are speaking; speaking the words

held up on cards now inside of
                    your head . . .

As then,
quite unexpectedly, at this point in time,
                    truth, it is discovered:
                    caught red-handed with
                    the cross

(and with a cripple biting down
hard upon it, as if to somehow
diminish your own pain).

You look up and see him, the imposter,
                    who has arrived finally (holding
                    out in front of his face your
                    face upon a stick),

                    has arrived, saying
                    (among other things):

'Think now of your church, life-size,
yet constructed of matchsticks and
consequently ready to crumble, if a
new and weighty-enough papyrus were
                    discovered . . .'

(Hands cupped around your own soul's
flame to protect it)

you ignore him.

And are imbued at last with the patience
needed to endure your own death.

– So maybe now, then, you have come to under-
stand everything?

Or perhaps you are only
a correct handshake away from going home?

But then suddenly from life's most ex-
cruciating stick you are hung;
the beam now that prevails over
your once inscrutable spine . . .

as your voice finally, it fades, or,
the echo of another voice, it stops

rebounding amid

the high vaults and
buttresses of your
skull . . .


III. VALEDICTION

So what's left now then to
emulsify into perfection?

Who has just woken up in
a room with nothing but the glossary
upon his bedside table?

– And how far still from home?

For there is not one face
left now in the universe

to attach your elated and
elastic-free mask to . . .

And instead of fear now, only the
question still of just who exactly
was it passed this sentence?

But to you here it makes now no
difference, for you have reached

it at last:

the crepuscular city.

Here
where now below you the sky
                    remains closed,
and the absent, they hang still
from hooks for a lack of skin . . .

But a place at last to speak of as your
                              own –

(with the obedient dropping now
finally from the parachutes of
their own souls into the clouds).

As your own body here beneath
you, it begins at last to drop.

And your soul, like a toy,
by your God, it is snatched right back
                    from you,

ending his long convalescence, after
religion . . .